The Caus
An Overture of Rebelli

Natalie McGrath is a playwright, song lyricist and Co-Director of Dreadnought South West. Following participation in the Hall for Cornwall's Responses Project in 2006/07, her first play *Metal Remains*, written for and produced by Theatre West in Bristol, was shortlisted for the Meyer Whitworth Prize. Her next full length play, *Coasting*, was commissioned and produced by Bristol Old Vic and was followed by *Scottish Kiss* for Paines Plough's Come to Where I'm From at Bristol Old Vic and *Wild Doves*, which was part of Bristol Old Vic's Short Fuses season. *Rift*, produced by the Brewhouse Theatre Taunton, was awarded the Inspire mark as part of the Cultural Olympiad 2012. *Exodus* was part of Box of Tricks Word: Play/NWxSW's cross-regional tour. *Oxygen*, for Dreadnought South West, toured along the route of the Great 1913 Women's Suffrage Pilgrimage from Land's End to Hyde Park, premiering at St. Just Town Hall, then touring to, among others, Theatre Royal, Plymouth, Exeter Phoenix at Rougemont Gardens, Carlton Theatre, Teignmouth, Yelde Hall, Chippenham and The Orange Tree in Richmond. Additional collaborations have included *Through the Wardrobe* for Exeter Northcott's Youth Theatre, *Etch* for Exim Dance, *This City's Centre* for Blind Ditch, and *Electric Spaces* for *We'll Meet in Moscow's* In Other Words, where she was also project lead. *In Tandem* was written for the Being Human Festival of Arts and Humanities. Natalie was an Associate at Exeter's Bike Shed Theatre and is an Associate Lecturer at the Department of Theatre and Performance at the University of Plymouth.

Dreadnought South West was founded by Josie Sutcliffe and Natalie McGrath in 2012 and became a charity in 2016. Its aim is to connect individuals and communities through telling great and courageous stories about women and girls, providing bold, high-quality arts and heritage work that inspires, educates and raises awareness throughout the South

West and beyond. Dreadnought's first major project – the new play *Oxygen* – celebrated and marked the centenary of the Great 1913 Women's Suffrage Pilgrimage, where women walked from Land's End to Hyde Park demanding their right to vote. Dreadnought's production of *Oxygen* toured throughout the South West, and in addition there were many arts and heritage way-marker projects led by individuals and communities along the route, inspired by the stories of women walking and protesting peacefully. It has been a model for Dreadnought's work ever since.

The Cause

An Overture of Rebellion and Revolt

By Natalie McGrath

With songs by Natalie McGrath,
Claire Ingleheart & Sarah Moody

Methuen

First published in paperback by Methuen 2018

1 3 5 7 9 10 8 6 4 2

Methuen
Orchard House
Railway Street
Slingsby, York, YO62 4AN

Methuen Publishing Limited Reg. No. 3543167

www.methuen.co.uk

A CIP catalogue record for this title is available from the British Library

ISBN: 978-0-413-77802-4

Typeset by SX Composing DTP, Rayleigh, Essex

Printed and bound in Great Britain by CPI Group (UK) Ltd, Croydon, CR0 4YY

Performance Rights Enquiries
All rights in this play are strictly reserved. A performance can be staged only once
a licence has been issued. All applications for performance must be submitted to
The Rights Department, Methuen (www.methuen.co.uk / rights@methuen.co.uk)
before rehearsals commence.

All forthcoming performance dates, administrative details and text
are correct the time of going to print.

The Cause

Produced by Dreadnought South West

Spring/Summer Tour 2018

The Cause was first performed on 25th & 26th April 2018 at Callywith College, Bodmin as part of intoBodmin and then at Crediton Arts Centre on 27th April 2018. Subsequent performances followed at the Acorn, Penzance on 3rd May, the Barbican Theatre, Plymouth from 10th to 12th May 2018, at Exeter Phoenix on 21st & 22nd May 2018, Ivor Potter Hall, Bude on 7th June 2018, St. Austell Arts Centre on 8th June 2018, Heartlands, Camborne on 9th June 2018, Yelde Hall, Chippenham on 15th & 16th June 2018, Redgrave Theatre, Bristol on 6th July 2018, The Lyric, Bridport on 10th July 2018 and Blackmore Theatre, Exmouth on 12th July 2018.

For details of the 2018 Autumn/Winter Tour please see:

www.dreadnoughtsouthwest.org.uk

Venues include South Devon College, Tacchi Morris Arts Centre, Teignmouth Pavilions, Tiverton Community Arts Theatre, Dartington Live, The Plough Torrington, Torquay Museum and The Regal Theatre, Minehead.

The final performance of *The Cause* tour will be at Exeter Phoenix on 14th December 2018.

The Cause on tour is funded by Arts Council England, Foyle Foundation, Exeter City Council, Fawcett Devon and the Ronald Duncan Foundation.

Thanks to Josie Sutcliffe for her outstanding dramaturgy & direction, to actors Michelle Ridings & Ruth Mitchell who have worked with us from the outset and to the audiences who supported the play's early stages of development at rehearsed readings.

All of you have made the writing of this play possible.

Original Cast:

Emmeline Pankhurst   Michelle Ridings

Millicent Fawcett   Ruth Mitchell

Trumpet   Remi Oriogun-Williams

Creative Team for *The Cause*:

Author & Song Lyricist: Natalie McGrath
Director/Dramaturg: Josie Sutcliffe
Musical Director: Sarah Moody
Film/Animation Artist: Catherine Cartwright
Filmmaker, PR & Marketing: Gillian Taylor
Costume Design & Making: Beth de Tisi
Set Design Consultant: Nicci Wonnacott
Choreographer: Diana Theodores
Movement Support: Belinda Chapman
Production Team: StS (Stage Technical Services)
Elaine Faulkner, Jamie Ransom, Amy Spencer & Will Tippett
Tour Manager: Kerrie Seymour
Evaluation: Mary Schwarz
Marketing & Audience Development: Mary Culhane
Designer: Nia Gould
Bookkeeper: Carly Macnamara
BSL Interpreter: Catherine Hall
Early music R&D & song 'Cut Glass': Claire Ingleheart
Script Development work: Saskia Portway & Hannah Kamen

Characters:

Emmeline Pankhurst   Leader of the militant Women's
                           Social and Political Union

Millicent Fawcett   Leader of the non-militant
                           National Union of Women's
                           Suffrage Societies

Trumpet   Dreamer / poet (from the
                           present) / singer of songs

Setting:

An orchard. Sometimes a prison cell. It is blurred.

It is June 1913 and **Emmeline Pankhurst** *is on the run.*

This is an imagined meeting.

Author's Note:

There is rhythm and pace in the staccato build. It is language moving forward. Always forward. Allow for gaps. Allow for space. Allow for moments to breathe.

Introduction

Bringing together Millicent Fawcett and Emmeline Pankhurst – two of the greatest leaders in the women's suffrage movement of the early 20th century – in an imagined meeting is a bold move by writer Natalie McGrath. *The Cause* speaks to issues that many people and, in particular, women and girls, face in our society today and highlights why it is an important new play.

Some may take issue with fiction replacing fact but something wonderful is happening here. We feel privy to possibility and hope, to love and respect: 'dirt and squalor as well as brilliance . . .' says Trumpet. It is rendered visceral and human, something that goes beyond established knowledge and leaves us wondering.

Too often the Suffragists, those law-abiding campaigners for equality and women's rights, played second fiddle to their more militant sisters the Suffragettes, the media being more interested in dramatic deeds than in the peaceful pilgrimages undertaken by the former. Beautifully and skilfully, Natalie redresses the balance through the dialogue between Emmeline and Millicent:

'This is how we are made visible . . . ,' says Emmeline in the play.

'It divides us, destroys us . . .' says Millicent.

Natalie, together with the female collaborating artists in the Dreadnought South West team, has delivered another kind of equality by shedding a very different light on this history using poetry and song, animation, movement, sound and rhythm. Each turn of the page, when brought to life onstage, reveals more depth and yet even more life, where the existence and beliefs of women over a century ago resonate loudly with the struggles of contemporary campaigners and activists. *The Cause* emphasizes the challenges a lifetime of campaigning can engender.

We have listened closely to audience feedback as we shared drafts of the script at readings during our development periods. Many of those who responded were activists themselves and their voices – fiercely embedded within the writing, the feel of the production and its trajectory – have played an important part of the dramaturgy of this work.

When audiences tell us that their experiences of the performances have proved intensely moving it makes the long haul of realizing the production of *The Cause* worthwhile. It may take time for *The Cause* to reach a wider audience, but its reverberations will be felt well into the future, thanks in part to this publication.

Josie Sutcliffe

The Cause

An Overture of Rebellion and Revolt

Part One

An orchard. Sometimes a prison cell. It is blurred. It is June 1913 and
Emmeline Pankhurst *is on the run. This is an imagined meeting.*

Trumpet

here we are

revolution
stings
the air

can you feel it?

it is everywhere

women
haunted
by a fervour
now they
see
another
way
to live

their stories
being
reconfigured

marching
battalions
forming
up
and
down
the land

voices

Trumpet (*cont.*)

on
makeshift
platforms
flooding
oratory
ground

lingering

the sound
of
women
making
noise

shattering
silence

here I am

a poet
a dreamer

there
could
be
worse
things

wondering
what
might
happen
if I
catch
this
current
tidal
wave

if I
take
a
long
leap

what
might
I see?

here they are

two great
women

leaders
from a
bygone
age

Millicent Fawcett
and
Emmeline Pankhurst

stuck
in time
on
vertiginous
currents
of air

driven together
by
unsteady
ground

one
walks
along

Trumpet (*cont.*) constitutional
lines
the other
heady
from
militant acts

one
is on
the run
the other
harbouring her
for just
a short
while

both lead their own armies

rail against the status quo

sacrificing
more
than we
can ever know

the crossfire is this

they are at odds
even though
they fight
for the
same
cause

to be
lawfully
recognised
as
citizens

to be
equal
and
protected
under law

to have
their
right
to vote

a battle not yet won

these
beacons
with
demands

shining brightly for so long

look at them

who are they
here
now
in private?

locked
in an
embrace
in this
wild wild
place

an ancient orchard

Millicent   your eyes
are
crystal clear

Millicent (*cont.*)   full of a blue
I never
witnessed
anywhere
else

of all the
faces
I have seen

looked into

this
is what
I remember
when I think
of you

Emmeline   they have been a great mask

Millicent   step into the light

Emmeline   look at me
shaking

Millicent   is it hurting your eyes?

Emmeline   wherever I go they block out the light

unseen

always a fugitive now

Millicent   you have
the elements
trapped
in your hair
wrapped
by stark

naked
summer light

Emmeline is it still June?

Millicent it is

Trumpet June 1913

Millicent the sun rises
impossibly
early

no time to dream

Emmeline I am being followed

Millicent you are safe here

Emmeline with you?

Millicent I am not interested in headlines

this is the
last place
they
would look

Emmeline can they lock you up for this?

Millicent I would like to see them try

Emmeline you
are
not
immune

what do you want?

Emmeline (*cont.*)   my mind is intact

                            be warned

Millicent   everything
                           here
                           is so ripe
                           so green
                           so ready
                           to startle
                           our senses

                           a canopy
                           so full
                           we
                           are
                           witnessing
                           nature
                           at
                           her
                           most alive
                           fit to
                           burst

                           look
                           at all
                           the shades
                           of colour
                           leaking
                           out

                           she
                           has been
                           generous
                           this
                           year

                           you
                           have been here before

Emmeline	have I?
Millicent	don't you remember?
	the deepest of echoes live here
	this is my orchard
Emmeline	it's better than the corner of a cell
	where geometry has subsided
	where time no longer exists
	why am I here?
Millicent	you sent me a note
Emmeline	did I?
	what did I say?
Millicent	'If I die what will you do?'
Emmeline	you didn't send one back
Millicent	then you didn't get it
Emmeline	what did you say?
Millicent	I said I would fight with my fists
Emmeline	liar
Trumpet	liar
	she's lying

Trumpet (*cont.*)   winding her up

Millicent   I am a liar

                            you know
                            I would never
                            use my fists
                            haven't used
                            my fists
                            since
                            I was a child

                            since
                            my sisters
                            and I
                            would play
                            together
                            here
                            in this orchard
                            fighting
                            over the apples
                            that fell
                            from the trees
                            to see
                            who
                            could collect
                            the most
                            to take
                            to our parents

                            another lifetime

Trumpet   look

                            she's over there

                            racing through the trees

                            she is wild

wilder than her sisters

the youngest of a tribe

look how she runs

her hair flying in the air

her arms
full of determination

look
how her lungs
occupy
the
world

it is how I imagine it

Millicent   I said
I would
continue
the fight
in my
own way

Emmeline   I'd better not die then

I could die

Millicent   you could

Emmeline   they won't let me die

Millicent   won't they?

Trumpet   I bet you

if she

Trumpet (*cont.*)   Emmeline
were to die
tomorrow

if they
were to cut her open

they would find
the word
revolution
written
across her organs

revolution

what a word it is

I love
the way
it sounds
as I say it
as it
rolls
off
my tongue

revolution

Emmeline   are we here
to celebrate
the fact
that I
am still alive?

Millicent   let me look at you

Emmeline   must you

everyone

wants to look at me

Millicent   it doesn't suit you

Emmeline   nothing suits me anymore

oh
you mean hunger striking

Millicent   you
are not a young woman

Emmeline   I am younger than you
by over a decade

that's a long time

Millicent   only if you are counting

Emmeline   I am counting

I have time
on my hands
wrapped
in a shawl
moving
from
place to place
inside the back
of a vehicle

a prisoner without her cell

this
this is paradise

Millicent   I see you now

your shape as sharp as a vine

Millicent (*cont.*)   taking centre stage
                               as a young woman
                               for the very first time

                               words
                               sing out
                               as you hit
                               every note
                               before
                               a sea of faces
                               expectant
                               wanting
                               searching
                               looking up
                               to you
                               as they
                               fall
                               fall deep
                               under
                               your
                               spell
                               fall
                               in love

Emmeline   you always were a romantic

                               it never helped

                     [*A nightingale's aria calls out*]

Emmeline   is it a nightingale?

Millicent   it is
                               it is a nightingale

Emmeline   it is tearing open the sky

listen

that note
how it
stretches out
the distance
harbouring
such
sadness

my mind

am I still a fugitive?

or am I locked in my cell?

Millicent

sometimes
I just don't know

Millicent
Emmeline
you
are here
in my orchard
where
no one else
can see

where
saplings soar
and
nightingales
sing arias
that weave
such magic
webs

Emmeline
there is

Emmeline (*cont.*)   no root
                          that can
                          break
                          or sprout
                          through
                          prison walls

                          prison knows nothing of nature

                          it has a nature
                          all of its own

Trumpet   never
                          underestimate
                          the violence
                          of nature

                          it is a force
                          unlike any other

                          look around

                          it will not stop
                          it will continue
                          long after
                          we are gone
                          after
                          we are
                          nothing
                          but shadows

Millicent   you are in shock

                          an apparition

                          I cannot bear to look at you

Emmeline   it's reckless
                          having me here

Millicent   don't speak to me of recklessness

Emmeline   tell me a story

                      you were
                      always so good at telling me
                      stories

Millicent   that was a long time ago

Emmeline   was it so long?

                      look at us

                      give me a story
                      give me something

                      stories
                      have been stolen from me

Millicent   at the edge
                      of the world
                      there is a valley
                      full of trees

                      harbouring
                      the labours
                      and injuries
                      of winter

                      it is frightened of letting go

                      of looking into the future

                      but knows it must take on this new dance

                      the valley begins to wonder
                      if it can muster strength

Millicent (*cont.*)   whether it can
live up to expectation

if it can find its voice once more

asking

will buds start to form?

will roots keep on holding fast?

what will
the earth provide us with now?

the valley is old

it thinks too much
cannot let
the things
it has witnessed
go
wondering
if it can watch
anymore lives
passing
through

one day
in the darkest pocket
of the life of the valley itself

as the faint glow
of sun
starts to shake

there is a sound

a sound that rivals
the magnitude of spring

it is like a low hum

and as the sun wakes up

carving through the valley
with orange lines

notes so fine

catching the creases of the earth
the hum gets louder

louder still

until a thin black line can be made out
in the distance

crossing through the sun's early flare

it is a signal

a signal has been sent to the valley

it is safe there
and so as the line
thickens
breathing
in its own rhythm

there are bees
bees
flying through air

they have
emerged with the sun

Trumpet   she
has

Trumpet (*cont.*)   brought
                          her
                          some
                          noise

Emmeline   I have longed for noise

                          silence
                          is a madness

                          your story
                          makes me think of wolves

Millicent   I always thought of you as a wolf

                          alone
                          at the top of a mountain

                          if I had to draw an image of you
                          that's what it would be

                          hunting

                          hunted

                          hurtling
                          towards
                          the end
                          of days

                          your body is so thin so worn
                          your body is like cut glass

                          I can count
                          the bones
                          in your hands
                          see arteries
                          I should not see

if you were
naked now
before me

I would see your heart beat
I would see your lungs expand and contract

Emmeline   stop it
stop it
stop it
stop it

I am prepared
to wrestle
the life out
of this body
until the earth
goes cold
around me
to see women
treated
with the respect
they deserve
valued as
rightful citizens

to exist

wrestle

are you?

too many words Millicent
too many

go on your
pilgrimage

Emmeline (*cont.*)   play with your hive
or whatever it is
you like to call it

not me

I remember being here

[*Song: Cut Glass*]

Trumpet   she remembers being here

with her
when her body moved faster
when her clothes
did not hang like relics
from another age

when her skin shone
and her smile sang

her body is so thin and worn
her body is like cut glass
her body is

she remembers being here

with her
walking shoulder to shoulder
side by side
sharing harmony
instead of rage

they were young then
restless like flames

her body is so thin and worn

her body is like cut glass
her body is

they remember being here

as they
took on the impossible
taking on the government
seeing
women being caged

and they fought like this
in a deep haze

her body is so thin and worn
her body is like cut glass
her body is

                              [*The song ends*

she cannot bear to look at her

Emmeline   my sisters
                    sing to us outside these walls

Millicent   we are not confined by any walls here

Emmeline   I want to
                    tear
                    them down
                    with my
                    bare hands

                    I am too weak to walk

                    my mind
                    is a cell
                    a trap
                    an illusion

Millicent   remember where you are

Emmeline   I cannot even raise my fist

                        are you trying to trick me?

Millicent   no it's me

                        it's Millicent

                        I am not your gaoler

Emmeline   I found
                        creases
                        in the walls
                        of my
                        prison cell
                        where
                        the names
                        of hundreds
                        of women
                        were
                        scratched
                        felt them
                        in my fingers
                        pressed them
                        against
                        the palms
                        of my hands
                        they were like
                        soft murmurs
                        lingering
                        in borders
                        rooted deep
                        in my
                        imagination
                        bringing
                        me comfort

Millicent   they're here with us now
                       in the bark of these trees

Trumpet   imagine that
                       if we
                       could do that

                       all those women

                       free to live
                       as they
                       choose

                       no longer
                       living
                       like
                       ghosts

                       I want to imagine them

                       walking
                       in
                       daylight

                       their hands
                       catching warmth

                       their faces
                       bending
                       towards
                       the light

                       their bodies
                       safe
                       at
                       last

                       I want to imagine them

Trumpet (*cont.*)   swimming in water
                              so clear

                              free to move
                              their limbs

                              catching
                              waves
                              that caress
                              their bodies

                              salt water
                              healing old wounds

                              the lull of the ocean
                              calming fears
                              catching
                              laughter
                              from
                              their
                              lungs

                              I imagine this

Emmeline   the wolves will save me

Millicent   Emmeline

                              there are no wolves here

Emmeline   before dawn
                              when I was
                              locked
                              in a cell
                              a small
                              feeling
                              in the curve
                              of my back
                              would start

a signal

I would wonder

is it
the beginning
of a new day?

will it be
identical
to the last?

is this fear
sliding its arms
slowly
around me?

gripping tightly
in this
horror chamber
where
darkness
and squalor
cling
to everything

I couldn't
remember
the beginning
or the end
of hunger
gnawing
away at me
asking me
to stop
telling me
how easy
it would be
to stop

Emmeline (*cont.*)   I heard
                            despair
                            inside
                            sounds

                            sounds
                            I did not know existed

                            only silence

                            that
                            barren place

                            I thought

                            can kill me now

Millicent   it is killing you

                            you have to stop
                            hunger striking

                            stop these
                            attacks
                            the violence
                            or they
                            will never
                            let you go
                            never stop
                            hounding you
                            never stop
                            sending you
                            back to prison

                            this
                            is killing you

                            this
                            act will kill you

Trumpet   women
                       too weak to stand

                       let alone
                       go on the run

                       the cruel
                       story
                       of the
                       government
                       cat
                       chasing
                       the
                       rebel mouse

Emmeline   you know
                       nothing
                       of violence
                       of sacrifice
                       to sacrifice
                       one's body
                       stomach
                       spine

Millicent   sacrifice?

                       you talk of it
                       as if you are
                       the only one

                       I have
                       forged
                       one alliance
                       after
                       another
                       in
                       government

                       I have

Millicent (*cont.*)   worked with diligence

                             I have fought

Emmeline   for what?

                             to be thought of
                             as if even you
                             do not have

                             'competent understanding'?

                             they have
                             done nothing but insult you

Millicent   then
                             I stand alone

Emmeline   poor Millicent
                             chip chip
                             chipping away
                             at the laws
                             men make
                             to suit
                             themselves

                             hoping that
                             men's words
                             will count
                             for something
                             sacred
                             knowing
                             deep inside
                             that they
                             won't

                             working out
                             routes
                             for women

to walk along

what good will that do?

we will be dead before anything changes

Millicent   attack me
if you like
with your
razor sharp
tongue

not my sisters

not women
who walk
peacefully

doing what is within their reach

walking
with all that they can muster

from the north
to the south
from the east
to the west

making
our cause
more visible
than it has
ever been

women
mapping this land

their bodies moving

Millicent (*cont.*)   together

their voices singing
in harmony

the insistent sound of women walking

if I put my ear to the ground
it is all I can hear

Emmeline   if I put my ear to the ground
I would never get up

Trumpet   it's true
look
at her

Millicent   I will tell you why
I keep my body
safe from harm

one of us has to

the cause needs one of us alive

you will be slaughtered
if you push much harder

Emmeline   shut up
shut up
shut up
shut the f**king f**k up

I know

it is my body
not yours

it is all I have left

Millicent   Emmeline

it is not all you have left

don't
leave me with this fight

for it is not won

it will not be won quickly
like you predict

don't you die
on me
not now

we are so close
to change

Emmeline   your
hope
is
misguided

betrays
us
all

Trumpet   these times

where
so much
anger
clouds
the
horizon

demand it

Emmeline   I am a warrior

                        what are you?

Millicent   someone who will not break the law

Emmeline   why do you think
                        they think
                        our lives
                        so meaningless?

Trumpet   is it
                        too deep
                        to
                        fathom
                        a
                        question
                        such
                        as this?

                        no

                        it must be answered

                        on
                        every
                        street
                        corner
                        in
                        every
                        country
                        across
                        every
                        continent

                        those
                        in
                        power
                        must

answer
this

Millicent   contempt
it is
contempt

Emmeline   it is fear

men fear women

men fear women having power

of having
what
they have
so
unquestionably

even
just a little bit of it

I will
not be owned

I belong to no one

where is your anger?

I remember
your anger
how it fired
my mind
captured
my
imagination

I take
one look at you now

Emmeline (*cont.*)   and
it is all
beneath
the veneer
your anger
is trapped
underneath
your skirt
inside
your dress
lining
the inside
of your skull
deep
in the flesh
we cannot see
longing
to be touched

how can you contain it?

Millicent   you have no restraint

Emmeline   I know

Millicent   stop trying to provoke me

Emmeline   what else is there to do?

here
we just talk

Trumpet   Emmeline
attacks
from the front
saying
no more delay

Millicent

works patiently
diligently
often out
of the limelight

both
are using
every fibre
they have
stretching
every muscle
on their
bones
raising
the
pace
of
their
hearts
tearing
themselves
apart

can't they see that?

Millicent

I remember
hiding behind
my mother's skirts
at my first
rally
those voices
still ringing
in my ears

my heart
swelling with pride
amidst
the excitement
of the crowd

Millicent (*cont.*)   fire in the speeches

I was young
just like you

around fourteen years old

that memory
for some
reason
hurts

maybe it's
because
there is
nothing else
in my blood
but this

I was
petitioning others
long before
I could sign
anything myself

like you
just like you

Emmeline   Millicent
I won't compromise

you
must know this
what ever it is
you want

I can't

Millicent   it divides us

destroys us

Emmeline   us?

what we achieved
together

it wasn't enough

we have not
done enough

gone
far enough

Millicent   I am afraid of what prison has done to you

Trumpet   it's a dance

they are
locked inside
this dance

at once
an embrace
at once
a fracturing
so
deep
of
fault lines
within
them
that
no one
else
can
see

Trumpet (*cont.*)

they are
wedded
to
one
another
like
old lovers
who
cannot
let go

belief
is on the line
and
belief
is everything
to them

they will
fight now

we are
walking
towards
a fight

even
the
orchard
knows
this

feels
this

these
rivals
from
different

tribes
will
fight

because
causes change

people change

Millicent   you speak as if it is a war

Emmeline   it is a war

Millicent   then it is a war you wage

Emmeline   a war
on women
is being
waged

my armies'
lungs
guts
tubes
are
being
massacred
behind
locked doors

this
is the price
my soldiers pay
lungs
that now
do not expand
so fast
or so slow
but

Emmeline (*cont.*)   just enough

we have
suffered
at the hands
of torturers
endorsed
by this
government

throats
that will now
always burn
from
forced feeding
reminding
them
always
of their cause

brilliant women

reduced
to
rubble

Millicent   but
death Emmeline

death
how can you bear it?

Emmeline   you
are obsessed by death

Millicent   what good
does martyrdom do?

Emmeline   I never felt so alive

when
I was so close
to death

Millicent

you mark
the battlefield
then

what
good
is
violence
against
violence?

when did it ever achieve anything?

this has become
your shell
your armour
look at you
your organs
rife with agony
your body
full
of bloody
rhythms
that will
not settle

Emmeline

I am not done
I am not done
I am not done yet

do not
mourn me yet

you tell me
then

Emmeline (*cont.*)   what is effective against this constant
                         drip of humiliation?

                         aren't you sick of it?

                         you're so calm

                         why are you so calm?

Millicent   you risk
                         the lives
                         of others
                         your soldiers
                         civilians
                         women

Emmeline   I would set fire
                         to the world
                         to have
                         the recognition
                         women
                         deserve

Millicent   you feed your army
                         your secret army this

                         young minds
                         ready
                         to worship
                         you
                         oh yes
                         I know
                         they think
                         you a saint

                         this is nothing
                         but
                         dangerous
                         irresponsible

propaganda

politicians
will not listen
whilst you
mark and burn
and scar
buildings

they
will not
listen
as you
fuel
rampant
arson
campaigns

if they will not
listen
as women
make
the ultimate sacrifice

look at what happened on Derby Day

Emmeline   don't you
touch
that nerve
she
Emily
was
my most
loyal of soldiers

I wasn't able to mourn her in public

Trumpet   look at Emmeline
blazing

Trumpet (*cont.*)   like midday sun

Emmeline   she had
                          our colours
                          wrapped
                          around
                          her body

Trumpet   what
                          must it
                          have
                          been like
                          to move
                          through
                          the noise
                          of that crowd
                          to slip
                          through it

                          unnoticed

                          to take that step out
                          out
                          out
                          into the swell
                          of
                          the race
                          the
                          danger

                          everything
                          moving
                          too fast
                          for the
                          human
                          eye

                          it shook their cause

shook them

Millicent   she was a great light

what a waste

Emmeline   shut up
you old crow
dressed
all in black
from
head to foot
as if you
were in
mourning
a permanent
state
of mourning

how dare you
speak of that

it is not yours to speak of
it is mine
not yours

it is
not over
not over
it is not
over yet

I will live long enough to see in my vote

will you?

I won't be a martyr

Millicent   won't you?

                       what good is glory?

Emmeline   I am radicalised
                       and there is
                       nothing
                       you can say
                       that will
                       make me
                       consider
                       law abiding
                       means

                       prison
                       has magnified my vision

                       everyone thinks me mad

                       I am not mad

                       nothing
                       moves minds
                       like the
                       smashing sound
                       of glass
                       or the
                       crack and splinter
                       of property
                       exploding
                       from
                       bombs

                       made by women

                       it is these sounds that make
                       governments listen

                       yes bombs

bombs
not the sounds of women walking

bombs

Trumpet   every
woman
on earth
could have
signed
a petition
declaring

'I want my right to vote I want it now'

and still
government
wouldn't
have
heard
them

Emmeline   there is nothing
nothing
at all
like the sound
of smashing
glass
the thrill
of lifting ones
arm
to strike
with my soldiers
at my side

what sound
better
challenges
ideas

Emmeline (*cont.*)   about women
and
obedience

as each splinter
flies through air
a symphony
is made
wild and free
from all authority

does your walking achieve any of this?

do your petitions make any difference?

Millicent   I cannot
accept
this
position
you take

they were
lucky
you were
lucky

those
recent
explosions
could have been
fatal

could you
live with that?

Emmeline   we have been
pushed

towards this
composition
pushed
pushed
pushed

nobody
has been
wounded
we never
intend
to wound

our violence is directed at property only

you know that

Trumpet   she does
Millicent knows this

although there
were some
close
calls

too
close
to
call

Millicent   do you
remember
visiting
a workhouse
for the
very
first time?

Millicent (*cont.*)   seeing
                               those young women
                               suffer

                               tiredness swollen into their feet

                               backs naked
                               bones showing
                               underneath skin
                               from labour
                               from poverty

                               we
                               witnessed
                               those
                               sub-human
                               conditions
                               women
                               and girls
                               were
                               subjected to

                               they
                               were
                               regarded
                               as
                               slaves
                               in
                               conditions
                               no one
                               should
                               endure

                               it continues
                               in our factories today

                               I still see their faces

                               remember what we fought for?

where we began

I am
still
fighting
for
that

we
are free

Emmeline   you are not free

you are a woman

Millicent   I will never
congratulate
you on
your bombs

this revolution
is one
that will be won
by stealth
diligence

measured grounds

I will fight for that

this
is how
change
will be
witnessed

Emmeline   I don't want to be a witness

I want to participate

Emmeline (*cont.*)   activate
agitate
agitate

I refuse
to be buried
a woman
who is not
considered
worthy
of her own
humanity

what is my mark
on this world
if I cannot achieve
this one thing?

it is too slow Millicent
too slow

Millicent   I am
one mark
on this world
and
you
are another

I am
not a violent woman

yet

I am
full of violence

like
spring
exploding

into
a rapture

you think me
rational
sane

you think me
calm

it is
a balancing act
all of this
between
sanity
and
and
slowly
going mad

underneath
my skin
words
are trapped
into membranes
so thin
jammed
into the joints
of my body
they are fierce
and sharp
like
the windows
your
sisters break

I use words
to attack
words

Millicent (*cont.*)   that fly
ignite
passion

words are how I sing

Emmeline   they are just words
Millicent

words

that flit across air
falling silently
like dust

stop cluttering everything with piety and
words

deeds
not
words

I will not live with disappointment

why do you?

Millicent   I am not disappointed

Emmeline   rubbish

Trumpet   she is
disappointed

Emmeline   I outstrip you
in this war

my army will strike
I will lead them
into

the most
dangerous
of battles

do not think
for one
minute
that they
will not
follow me

watch as
my
young
hot bloods
strike

wreaking
havoc
on bricks
and mortar

upon
property
private
property

it is all
governments
really
care for

I have
my army

where is yours?

Millicent   I have my hive
full of industry

Millicent (*cont.*)   I will listen to it

                              I will listen
                              to my hive
                              full of purpose
                              common
                              cause

                              they are
                              mobilised
                              my battalions
                              outnumbering
                              your
                              militants

                              on foot

                              law abiding
                              suffragists
                              in their tens
                              of thousands

                              ready to march

                              ready to move
                              united
                              in their masses

                              they will
                              march
                              soon
                              soon
                              they will
                              march

Trumpet   both of them use this language of war

                              Millicent
                              doesn't care for it

I can feel that

even though
it marks
her
vocabulary

I wonder

what was the alternative?

Millicent   this loathsome language of war
I use

I do not recognise myself

Emmeline   it is what men hear

Trumpet   shame

it is what they hear

Millicent   what a pity

Emmeline   this
is how we become visible in the world

Millicent   it makes me feel ashamed

who keeps
the peace
in the wake of
your actions

who sits
and waits
whilst
committee
after committee

Millicent (*cont.*)   permits
                               some slither of hope
                               only to spit me
                               back out
                               because
                               your artillery
                               booms
                               in the
                               background

                               as you race
                               ahead
                               fly wildly
                               above us all
                               constitutional ground
                               doesn't get
                               challenged

Emmeline   f**k 'the constitution'
                               let us rip it up
                               make something new

Millicent   yes
                               f**k 'the constitution'

                               those bastards
                               will never capitulate

                               better
                               to set it on fire
                               better
                               to burn down
                               buildings
                               better
                               to come close
                               to murder
                               attack property
                               attack
                               what they

consider
rightfully
theirs

attack everything then because they own it all

come on Emmeline

Emmeline   you moderate

Millicent   you call me moderate
like it is a slander
I feel it fizz off your tongue
full of condescension
as if you use it
as the butt
of a joke

is it a joke?
is it?

don't make fun of me

it doesn't make us equal

Emmeline   you're
a different colour now

Millicent   anger
is not your exclusive right

Emmeline   here is a stone
pick it up
feel its weight
in the palm
of your hand

no?

Emmeline (*cont.*)   take it from me
                          go on
                          why be
                          so obedient Millicent

                          take it
                          take it

Millicent   you hit me
                          with
                          one note
                          one note
                          one note

                          have you
                          forgotten
                          what it is to fight
                          with
                          non-violence?

                          have you?

                          I put one foot in front of the other

                          keep
                          a momentum
                          keep moving
                          keep the muscles
                          in my body active
                          until they ache

                          I have to keep moving

                          no time to stop
                          otherwise
                          it reminds me
                          that
                          being reasonable
                          has driven me

to the point
of
collapse

day
after day
after day
after day
after day
after day
after day
after day
after day
after day
after day
after day
after day
after day
after day
after day
after day
after day
after day
after day
after day
after day
after day
after day
after day
after day
after day
after day
after day
after day
after day
after day
after day
after day
after day
after day

Millicent (*cont.*)   after day
after day
after day
after day
after day
after day
after day
after day
after day
after day
after day
after day
after day
after day
after day
after day
after day
after day
after day
after day
after day
after day
after day
after day
after day
after day
after day
after day
after day
after day
after day
after day
after day
after day
after day
after day
after day
after day
after day
after day
after day
after day
after day

after day
after day
after day
after day
after day
after day
after day
after day
after day
after day
after day
after day
after day
after day
after day
after day
after day
after day
after day
after day
after day
after day
after day
after day
after day
after day
after day
after day
after day
after day

after day

after day

some days I feel like I could destroy everything

I don't know

Millicent (*cont.*)   what to do
                               with my
                               moderation

                               because
                               inside
                               I rage
                               and
                               I burn

                               just like you

                               just like you

                               so it takes
                               every ounce of me
                               to say

                               I will not
                               pick up
                               that stone
                               that you
                               taunt me
                               with

                          [*Silence. Absolute silence.*]

Trumpet   these
                               moments
                               make
                               a circumference
                               of air
                               where air
                               should
                               not be
                               find
                               deliverance

in cracks
in the ground
sending out
ripples
across time
reaching
out
to
dimensions
not yet
found

what will be saved from the wreckage of this?

[*Sounds of smashing glass against bees*]

The Cause

An Overture of Rebellion and Revolt

Part Two

[Song: When Courage Calls to Courage]

Trumpet   when courage
                         calls
                         to courage

                         do not
                         do not
                         let her
                         voice
                         be
                         denied

                         when rebel
                         calls
                         to rebel

                         do not
                         do not
                         let her
                         voice
                         be
                         denied

                         let the pane of glass break
                         let the paths be worn thin
                         let the sound of resistance boom

                         let freedom be called out loud

                         when woman
                         calls
                         to woman

                         do not
                         do not
                         let her
                         voice

Trumpet (*cont.*)   be
                          denied

                          when anger
                          calls
                          to anger

                          do not
                          do not
                          let her
                          voice
                          be denied

                          let the pane of glass break
                          let the paths be worn thin
                          let the sound of resistance boom

                          let freedom be called out loud

                          when action
                          calls
                          to action

                          do not
                          do not
                          let her
                          voice
                          be
                          denied

                          when sister
                          calls
                          to sister

                          do not
                          do not
                          let her
                          voice
                          be

denied

let the pane of glass break
let the paths be worn thin
let the sound of resistance boom

let freedom be called out loud
let freedom be called out loud
let freedom be called out loud

let freedom be called out loud

                       [*The song ends*

she said that

Millicent
said
'when
courage
calls to
courage'

that howl
before
from the pit
of her
stomach

that
sound so raw
that
we all heard

is that the
sound
everywoman
makes

when we

Trumpet (*cont.*)   hit
the floor

when we
push
for so long

these
warriors
have
knocked
me
off
my perch

I find myself
falling
then
I find myself
wildly
awake
in a
heightened
state
and
then
again
before
me
a
new
landscape

shining
brightly
like
the sun

I hear

them
through
the ages

I hear
them
on the
ocean floor

I hear
them
in the
skies above

I hear
them
quietly
opening
the door

Millicent   I am not your enemy

Emmeline   release me
                       then
                       back
                       into the wild

Millicent   I am sixty-six years old

                       I am tired

                       I have been
                       campaigning
                       for fifty years

Trumpet   fifty years

                       fifty years

Millicent   everything has worn very thin

                           look at my fists
                           they are
                           gnarled
                           like the base
                           of these
                           ancient trees

                           it is
                           a long haul

                           yes

                           this is
                           the long haul

                           I am in it
                           for the longest haul

                           we are in it

Trumpet   this
                           place
                           full
                           of pain
                           is
                           an
                           energy
                           a
                           wide
                           reaching
                           current
                           an
                           electrical
                           storm
                           connecting
                           us
                           all

Millicent

you think
you are
the only
radical here

the only one
engaged
in a battle

we
are both on the frontline

Emmeline

I need you
to
stay alive

stay alive

the cause
needs you
to do
this
one
thing

Trumpet

how many
women
have fallen
on these
battlegrounds?

have
been
on
hunger
strike?

Trumpet (*cont.*)   have
                               been
                               beaten
                               on the
                               street?

                               how many
                               are
                               imprisoned
                               with
                               no
                               right
                               to
                               fight?

                               have
                               stared
                               down the
                               barrel
                               of a
                               gun?

                               how many?

Emmeline   after
                               she
                               fell foul
                               to police
                               brutality

                               I thought I might lose my mind

                               such petty
                               vindictive
                               assaults

                               wanting
                               to crush us
                               out of

existence

after
the swell
of the crowd
I lost sight
of her

lost sight
of
so many
of
my soldiers

women
dispersed
by violence

I thought
I might
kill
someone
from grief

I felt
responsible
as I led
that day

a simple
petition
to parliament
ending
in injuries
that some
women
never
recovered
from

Emmeline (*cont.*)   women
in wheelchairs
left lying
face down
in alleyways

women
dragged
along
by their hair
in the street

being
separated
shoved
into vans

it has
become
so dark
in my
mind
Millicent

always there
haunting me

darker than the cell

darker than
day eight
of
hunger striking
when
your mind
starts
to wander
in and out
of itself

when
there
was
nothing
tangible
of me
left

I remember
being
beaten
that day

my breasts
were
black and blue
and me
left
wondering

Trumpet   who
would do
such
a thing
as this?

who
would
allow
such
a
thing?

Emmeline   that was the darkest day
for me

Black Friday
was a
battlefield

Emmeline (*cont.*)   I saw
the cost
understood
the risk
in a
new way
and
I
haven't
looked
back

Millicent   no one
could
believe
what
happened

it was
the darkest of days

the
world shuddered

filling full of shame

Trumpet   this
shocking story
that
history
has forgotten

this injustice
from long ago
that began
with names
carefully
written
in ink

onto
paper

it is
not
taught
in
schools

it
has
been
erased

these stories
are carried
around
in silence

silence

but the violence

it's still
the same

it's still
the same

the distance
they
are
trying
to reach
pushing
so hard
towards

we

Trumpet (*cont.*)   aren't there yet

we
aren't there yet

we
aren't there

Emmeline   don't
come near me

it is
before dawn
that
I see her now
with
all
the other
ghosts
the other
women
whose health
has been lost
to this cause
whose lives
have
been lost
to violence

it is inside here

inside
these moments

that I
plan bombs

this
is the sacrifice I make

it is here
my humanity
dwindles

I want freedom

freedom or death

there is
no surrender
now
from this

your frontline
and my
frontline
are not
the same
no matter
what
you may think
because
they are not
the same
in here

Millicent   I plant trees
to mark
your sacrifice

every
part of me
feels
the irony
in this

every
part of me
is made

Millicent (*cont.*)   of a different
                                political metal
                                to you

                                why is that?

                                something
                                that keeps
                                me fixed
                                immoveable

                                I cannot explain it

                                I don't believe in violence
                                I just don't

                                I believe in diplomacy

                                I believe in
                                purposeful
                                movement

                                in my hive

                                its industry

                                this is who I am

Trumpet   she is
                                more than this

                                we have
                                seen it
                                felt it

                                she is
                                so much
                                more
                                than we

can
know

Millicent   if a woman
can only
show her
resistance
by walking
ten yards
or
one hundred
yards
or be
listening in
at the back
of a crowd
unseen

if that
is her only
contribution
to the cause
according to her
circumstances
then so be it
for it is
circumstance
that we are
working
towards
changing

I know you know this

Trumpet   she does
she does know this

Millicent   the frontline
is an ever

Millicent (*cont.*) changing
thing
for me

Emmeline that rage

it felt good
didn't it?

Millicent it did

it did

Emmeline what will you do with it now?

Millicent I don't know

Emmeline I am tired Millicent

I want it to be done

I want it to be done

Trumpet they
can see one another now

I see them now
in new light

reverence
and
shadows
start
to form

they're ghosts

there is dirt and squalor in their minds

as well
as
brilliance

I was
not
prepared
for
this

nothing
looks
or
feels
the
same

this
body
this
mind
this
life
that
I inhabit
has
choices
to
make

Emmeline   I could thrive in this orchard

can I stay?

let them
get on with it
without us

Millicent   it heard you

Millicent (*cont.*)   see
                              see
                              the trees
                              sway
                              they are
                              making
                              that
                              gentle
                              sound

                              nature's
                              cycles
                              rumbling
                              on
                              as we
                              turn
                              to dust

                              ever
                              expanding
                              harmony
                              gently
                              lulling me
                              to here
                              always
                              to here

                              I can feel it

                              this
                              symphony
                              between us
                              is so acute

                              it is a pity there is so little time

                              I
                              cannot
                              absorb

its
notes

Trumpet   there
is
something
close
to
love
here

Millicent   Emmeline

I do not
think you mad

I never met
anyone
with such
fire
and clarity

stay
as long as you like

as long as it is safe

Emmeline   will we meet again?

Millicent   not like this

you
rouse
too much
passion
in me

Emmeline   I am glad I rouse passion in someone

Millicent   my heart cannot take it

Trumpet   they won't
                           meet again
                           like this

                           the conflict
                           is too great
                           it is written
                           into time
                           they will never
                           meet again
                           like this

                           suffragette
                           suffragist

                           militant
                           non-militant

                           rivals

                           pioneers

                           rebels

Emmeline   then
                           we will march on

                           without
                           one
                           another

                           at least
                           now
                           I remember
                           who
                           you are

Millicent   I would like to be buried here

Emmeline   if you beat me to it

                     I will make sure of it

Millicent   is that a promise?

Emmeline   as close to one as you will ever get
                     from me

                     I'll put
                     'deeds not words'
                     on your
                     gravestone

Millicent   you wouldn't dare

Emmeline   I wouldn't dare

                     I'll let the hive handle that

Millicent   I miss this

                     intimacy

                     I have
                     been alone
                     for too
                     long

                     I miss everything

Emmeline   I refuse
                     to be alone

                     all this nature
                     makes me
                     think

Emmeline (*cont.*)   about sex

Millicent   I miss sex

Trumpet   good answer Millicent

Emmeline   I enjoy sex

Millicent   nothing you say can shock me now

Emmeline   did I push too hard?

Trumpet   she
                         has
                         shadows
                         lurking
                         inside
                         her eyes

                         they were buried deep

                         now
                         she
                         looks
                         haunted

Millicent   all
                         this
                         fighting
                         makes
                         me
                         so
                         lonely

Emmeline   has this fight not been enough for you?

                         has it not kept
                         your
                         blood warm?

filled every hour
of every
waking
moment?

driven
your
dreams
to
despair?

brought
you
the
company
of
brilliant
women?

Millicent there
has
been
no time
to think
about
being
held

Emmeline

it has
taken
the years
from
underneath
us

Trumpet they
have

Trumpet (*cont.*)   so little
time
together

a fragment

what
they don't
know
is this

a bigger
force
than them
is coming
bigger
than they
could
have
imagined

slaughter
on a scale
never
witnessed
before

catastrophe

a different
kind
of war
is coming

a new version
of hell
is on
their horizon
ready to

stop
them
in
their
tracks

war

shaking
the
earth
to its
core

Millicent   the day
is heaving now

look at it

we have
met
amidst
these
luscious
trees

I am
at home
here

that
is something

these blades
of grass
will tickle
and tear
at our feet

Millicent (*cont.*)   take
off your shoes

I am going to take off mine

Trumpet   look at you Millicent

will she follow her
in this one thing?

this
declaration
of love
for the
earth

will
it last?

or will
cruel time
have
the last
laugh?

I'm taking off mine

Millicent   come on
come on

feel the earth beneath you

forget
forget
for one moment

forget
that
anything

else exists

close your eyes

feel the earth

Emmeline   I surrender
                     to this one and only thing

Trumpet   a vote
                     not won
                     for
                     some
                     until
                     1918

                     a vote
                     not won
                     for
                     all
                     until
                     1928

                     how did they bear it?

                     this is for them
                     this is for you

[*Song: This is The Cause*]

                     lift up
                     your head
                     as
                     shadows fall

                     raise up
                     your fist

Trumpet (*cont.*)

as
the cause
calls

lift up
your voice
as
dreams collide

raise up
your fist
as
the cause
calls

tear down
the walls
that
make you
hide

tear down
the lies
that
make
you
survive

this is
the cause

it's mine
and
it's yours

this is
the cause

it's mine

and
it's yours

lift up
your heart
as
poetry flies

raise up
your fist
as
the cause
calls

lift up
your soul
as
the tide turns

raise up
your fist
as
the cause.
calls

tear down
the walls
that
make you
hide

tear down
the lies
that
make
you
survive

this is

Trumpet (*cont.*)   the cause

it's mine
and
it's yours

this is
the cause

it's mine
and
it's yours

lift up
your dreams
as
love survives

raise up
your fist
as
the cause
calls

lift up
your hope
as
women rise

raise up
your fist
as
the cause
calls

tear down
the walls
that
make you

hide

tear down
the lies
that
make
you
survive

tear down
the walls
that
make you
hide

tear down
the lies
that
make
you
survive

this is
the cause

it's mine
and
it's yours

this is
the cause

it's mine
and
it's yours

this is
the cause

Trumpet (*cont.*)   it's mine
                               and
                               it's yours

                               this is
                               the cause

                               it's mine
                               and
                               it's yours

                                                    [*The song ends*

Emmeline   I have earth between my toes

                               look at me

                               what
                               would it be
                               to have all
                               the seasons
                               in one day
                               one hour
                               one minute

                               a second

                               I cannot
                               recall
                               when I last
                               did
                               something
                               like this

                               was I a child?

                               I must have been a child

                               how could you?

Millicent

Millicent   there are
          butterflies
          flitting
          in and out

          such a sharp
          pang of blue
          across green

          look

          you are not looking

Emmeline   it is
          too soon for blues

          is it an omen?

          when will they come for me?

Millicent   soon
          soon

          too soon

          the imagination hurts
          doesn't
          it?

Emmeline   it is a refuge

Millicent   what
          did you think
          about the
          Stravinsky
          music
          that

Millicent (*cont.*)   caused a riot
                                 in Paris?

                                 were you there?

                                 now

                                 I should
                                 have liked
                                 to have
                                 witnessed
                                 that
                                 by
                                 your
                                 side

The Cause

An Overture of Rebellion and Revolt

Songs

Cut Glass

Natalie McGrath

Claire Ingleheart

When Courage Calls to Courage

Natalie McGrath

Sarah Moody

This is the Cause

Voice

Natalie McGrath

Sarah Moody

Lift up your head   as sha-dows fall___   raise up your fists   as the

cause calls___   lift up your voice   as dreams coll ide___   raise up your

fists   as the cause calls   Tear down the walls that   make you hide

tear down the lies that make you sur-vive   This is the cause it's mine and it's yours

This is the cause it's mine and it's yours   Lift up your heart

as po-et ry flies   raise up your fists   as the cause calls___

lift up your soul   as the tide turns   raise up your fist   as the

cause calls   Tear down the walls that   make you hide   tear down the lies that

make you sur - vive   This is the cause it's   mine and it's yours

This is the cause it's   mine and it's yours

Voice